The Month of Christmas Dreams

Written by
Dr Phillip & Meghan Deam

Foreword

The month of December has always been a special time for our little family. There's something magical about the way the world transforms, as homes and streets begin to sparkle with Christmas lights and decorations. One of our favorite traditions is bundling up the kids and driving through the neighborhood, marveling at the glowing lights and festive displays.

As the days pass and Christmas Eve approaches, the excitement in our home reaches its peak. The anticipation of Santa's arrival, the stories told by the fireplace, and the quiet moments spent together remind us all of the joy that the season brings. It's not just about the presents or the decorations; it's the closeness that Christmas creates—the laughter, the shared moments, and the love that fills the air.

Phillip Dean

Oh my, December is here,
It's almost Christmas, our favorite time of year.

There's Henry and Charlie and now Ivy too,
They've waited all year, for their Christmas wish to come true.

They've been nice, they've been naughty,
but mostly they've been good.

Dreaming of presents,
as any child would.

The tree is decorated with precision and care,
They're so happy that Santa soon will be there.

He's so jolly and happy in his fury red coat,
his rosy cheeks glow, with a smile that brings hope.

The stocking hang by the mantle with grace,
Each one a symbol of Santa's warm embrace.

The month of December, sees streets filled with bright lights,
and snow tops the trees, as we drive through the night.

Houses are covered with garlands galore,
and rooftops are covered as Frosty adorns.

Icicles glisten, and lights brightly shine,
Creating a scene that's simply divine.

The children write their Christmas letters,
to old St Nick.
Then place them in the fire,
they travel so quick.

The smoke carries their wishes,
up into the clouds.
Our parents say,
we must have any doubts.

They whisper their hopes,
and send them above.
Trusting in Santa,
their hearts full of love.

It's now christmas eve,
the fireplace roars.
Daddy sits with his night cap,
the kids giggle as he snores.

They try to lay awake,
to hear Santa's sleigh.
But asleep they all fall,
in front of the fire they lay.

Dreams of tomorrow,
fill each little head.
As the magic of Christmas,
surrounds each bed.

The fire light dances,
casting shadows that play.
As we dream of Santa,
and his magical sleigh.

The world outside,
is covered in snow.
In our hearts,
the true spirit of Christmas does grow.

Tonight, we are wrapped,
in a blanket of love.
Under the watchful gaze,
of Santa above.

Merry Christmas everybody

Phillip & Meghan Deam

www.ingramcontent.com/pod-product-compliance
Lightning Source LLC
Chambersburg PA
CBHW042359070526
44585CB00029B/2999